Makerspace Careers™

CAREERS IN

MANUFACTURING

JESSICA SHAW

Rosen
YA™
New York

Published in 2020 by The Rosen Publishing Group, Inc.
29 East 21st Street, New York, NY 10010

First Edition

Library of Congress Cataloging-in-Publication Data

Names: Shaw, Jessica, 1972– author.
Title: Careers in manufacturing / Jessica Shaw.
Description: First edition. | New York, NY : The Rosen Publishing
Group, Inc., 2020. | Series: Makerspace careers | Includes bibli-
ographical references and index. | Audience: Grades 7–12.
Identifiers: LCCN 2018048759| ISBN 9781508188100 (library
bound) | ISBN 9781508188094 (pbk.)
Subjects: LCSH: Manufacturing industries—Vocational guidance—
Juvenile literature. | Manufacturing processes—Juvenile literature.
Classification: LCC TS183 .S475 2020 | DDC 338.4/767023—dc23
LC record available at https://lccn.loc.gov/2018048759

Manufactured in China

CONTENTS

INTRODUCTION

"Manufacturing" is defined as making something from raw materials. The first human ancestors to make weapons, jewelry, clothes, and artwork were essentially pioneers of the manufacturing industry. As civilizations have evolved, so have the products being manufactured. Anything and everything that is in demand at any given time—that is, anything that people want or need—must be manufactured by someone. Since there is no foreseeable end to the number or types of products people will want or need, there will most certainly always be a demand for manufacturers. To manufacture is to make, and in one way or another, everyone is a maker, whether or not they sell the products they produce. More than ever before, schools, libraries, businesses, teachers, parents, and communities are encouraging current and future generations of makers, providing spaces specifically designed to inspire and equip people who would like to try their hand at creating. These spaces are commonly referred to as makerspaces and the collective energy and support fueling this transformative phenomenon in communities around the world have come to be known as the maker movement.

Widely regarded as the father of the maker movement, Dale Dougherty has been honored as a White House Champion of Change and recognized as a significant American innovator by President Barack Obama. In 2005, Dougherty launched *Make:* magazine, which

Beginning with the earliest civilizations, people have been innovators and makers, producing everything from weapons, tools, and utensils to pottery, jewelry, and art.

features step-by-step projects, skill-building lessons, and inspirational articles from successful makers. The launch of the magazine was followed by a series of fun maker events around the globe called Maker Faires. Dougherty's magazine and Maker Faire events shined a spotlight on the creative spirit of makers and the incredible benefits to makers and to society as a whole when that creative spirit is encouraged and allowed to flourish. In 2009, Obama launched the Educate to Innovate campaign, stating, "I want us all to think about new and creative ways to engage young people in science and engineering, whether it's science festivals, robotics competitions, fairs that encourage young people to create and build and invent—to be makers of things, not just consumers of things." Institutions such as schools, libraries, and museums have answered the call, allocating time, space, and resources for aspiring young creators.

Makerspaces are places where people with shared interests in things like technology, computing, design, engineering, and art can gather to work on projects, either individually or collaboratively, while sharing equipment and knowledge and enjoying the added benefit of bouncing ideas off one another. A makerspace can be as simple as an area for young builders and creators equipped with LEGOs, cardboard, and art supplies or as sophisticated as a workshop equipped with a variety of laser cutters, soldering irons, 3D printers, computer numerical control (CNC) machines, welders, saws, sanders, drills, and sewing machines. For those interested in a career in manufacturing, the hands-on time spent working in a makerspace can be an invaluable experience. The type of equipment found in many makerspaces is similar to equipment commonly used in manufacturing facilities. Before makerspaces, opportunities for people to learn how to use such advanced equipment were limited to advanced coursework in specialized technical courses or on-the-job training. Now, thanks to makerspaces, those eager to land a great job in manufacturing can gain experience in the field before ever setting foot on a jobsite!

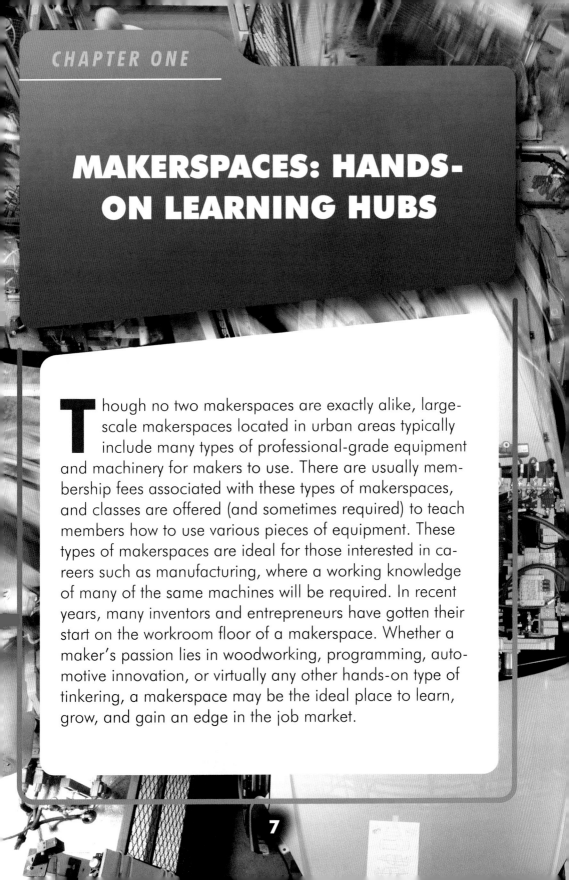

CHAPTER ONE

MAKERSPACES: HANDS-ON LEARNING HUBS

T hough no two makerspaces are exactly alike, large-scale makerspaces located in urban areas typically include many types of professional-grade equipment and machinery for makers to use. There are usually membership fees associated with these types of makerspaces, and classes are offered (and sometimes required) to teach members how to use various pieces of equipment. These types of makerspaces are ideal for those interested in careers such as manufacturing, where a working knowledge of many of the same machines will be required. In recent years, many inventors and entrepreneurs have gotten their start on the workroom floor of a makerspace. Whether a maker's passion lies in woodworking, programming, automotive innovation, or virtually any other hands-on type of tinkering, a makerspace may be the ideal place to learn, grow, and gain an edge in the job market.

Makerspaces are becoming welcome additions to many urban areas around the world, offering creators the space, tools, and resources they need.

CRAFTSMANSHIP 101: WOODWORKING

Woodworking enthusiasts will find a variety of hand tools and power tools to work with in makerspaces. These may include many types of saws such as table saws, compound miter saws, band saws, and scroll saws. CNC wood routers, table routers, and shapers are tools used in makerspaces to hollow out (rout) an area in wood to create a pattern or decorative edge. A mortiser is a specialized woodworking machine used to cut square or rectangular holes in a piece of lumber, whereas a drill press is a machine tool used for drilling standard holes. Another standard piece of woodworking equipment in makerspaces is a lathe. A lathe is a machine tool that rotates a piece of wood while various operations such as cutting, sanding, and drilling are performed with tools that are applied to the wood. Belt or disc sanders are also standard fare in makerspaces and are used to create a smooth, finished wood surface. Makerspace woodworking projects are limited only by a maker's imagination. Wooden toys, artwork, and jewelry are a few small-scale projects that can be completed with or without collaboration, while larger projects, including trim work and custom pieces of furniture such as tables, chairs, bookshelves, dressers, cabinets, drawers, and doors are also possibilities in a well-equipped makerspace.

3D PRINTING

Many makerspaces, including those in schools and libraries, offer users the opportunity to create products with a 3D printer. Also referred to as additive manufacturing, 3D printing is a process of creating a three-dimensional solid object from a digital file. The processes used in the creation

With many school campuses now providing well-equipped maker-spaces, students have greater access to state of the art machines such as 3D printers.

of 3D-printed objects are known as additive processes because layer upon layer is added during printing. The object is created when enough layers of material have been added to precisely form the object.

More and more, librarians, teachers, and professors are recognizing the benefits of 3D printers and integrating them into their classrooms and makerspaces. Students are developing problem-solving skills as they are challenged to develop prototypes that fill a need or meet certain criteria to 3D print. Coming up with ideas fuels creativity, and seeing their hard work pay off as the object they created comes to life in the 3D printer is a rewarding and motivating experience that inspires students to see what they can create next. The potential applications for 3D printing are exciting, to say the least, with 3D-printing projects such as food, housing, art exhibits, prosthetic limbs and organs, and even automobile parts currently underway in makerspaces, engineering labs, hospitals, museums, and manufacturing and research facilities around the world.

PROBLEM SOLVING WITH PROGRAMMING

From apps and video games to innovative applications and graphics software, there's really no limit to the problem solving that can be accomplished through programming. Makerspaces might be equipped with only a basic computer workstation, or they might include a computer lab with an impressive array of all the latest equipment. Aspiring programmers enjoy the challenge of learning

SQUARE: A MAKERSPACE SUCCESS STORY

Not long ago, budding inventors with cutting-edge ideas were often stymied by a lack of equipment or necessary funding to develop a prototype and move forward with their inventions. With the introduction of makerspaces, suddenly people had access to the tools, equipment, and work spaces they needed to create working prototypes. One well-known invention that was developed in

Inventions such as the credit card reader Square dongle have enabled many creators to open their own small businesses and accept payments on the go.

a makerspace and became a roaring success was the popular credit card reader Square. A prototype of the Square dongle was developed in 2010 by James McKelvey after his business partner, Jack Dorsey, came up with the idea. The small, square-shaped device attaches to mobile devices through the headphone jack and allows users to swipe a credit card and enter an amount to accept as payment. By simplifying the process of accepting credit card payments, Square has helped many other makers, inventors, and entrepreneurs grow their own businesses. From a small plastic prototype to a mainstream payment-processing device, Square is a makerspace success story that today is valued in the billions!

programs as well as developing innovative solutions to everyday problems, and a makerspace offers the environment and equipment needed to pursue those programming challenges. Equipment used by programmers that is frequently found in a makerspace includes computers with large monitors, color printers, scanners, and copiers, as well as advanced engineering software, design and editing software, and CNC programming software.

AUTOMOTIVE AND ASSEMBLY WORK

Those who enjoy working on all things engine, automobile, or assembly will be happy to know that there are many makerspaces equipped with an impressive array of tools and equipment to aid in those pursuits. Standard automotive equipment and tools often found in makerspaces include work bays with auto lifts and engine hoists, floor jacks and jack stands, specialty automotive tools, hand tools, air tools, alignment tools, battery chargers, and diagnostic computer equipment and scanners. Makerspaces do not usually allow users to store automobiles on-site overnight, but some have outdoor space that can be reserved for that purpose. Whether replacing a leaky hose or building an engine from scratch, there are well-equipped makerspaces with everything an aspiring mechanic might need.

Assembly work areas in makerspaces might include equipment such as worktables, vises, compressed air machines, any number of hand and portable power tools, and a variety of remnant materials that are shared among makerspace users. These areas are ideal for working on a project with a group of people or for laying out projects with many parts and steps.

EQUIPMENT OPERATOR SKILLS: MACHINING

A machinist is someone who uses machine tools to produce or modify metal parts to suit many different types of industrial applications. In machining, ultraprecise measurements are crucial, as deviations of even a miniscule amount can mean the difference between a part that functions as it should and one that doesn't function at all. Machining equipment and tools commonly available in makerspaces includes CNC milling machines, metalworking lathes, shaper machines, drill press machines, calipers, micrometers, edge finders, squares, telescoping gauges, wrenches, hammers, center punches, magnet sets, grinding wheels, files, and sanders. Machinists can create specific parts for a piece of equipment or machinery, from a small bicycle part or industrial valve to complex pieces such as magnet core assemblies for particle accelerators and intricate prototype parts. Some machinists also use their skills to create works of art from pieces of metal. Most machining projects involve turning a piece of some kind of metal into an object or a part through skilled operation of many types of metalworking machines and hand tools.

THE ART OF WELDING

Welding and metal fabrication can give rise to any number of creative projects in a makerspace. There are different areas of specialty within the field of welding, such as gas metal arc welding (MIG welding), gas tungsten arc welding (TIG welding), and shielded metal arc welding. Makerspaces generally have equipment such as MIG welders, TIG welders, electric welders, oxygen and acetylene torches, and plasma cutters. Metal-fabrication equipment includes grinders, chop saws, band saws, and belt and disc sanders. Welding is truly an industrial art form, one that requires quite a bit of special training

Welders are in great demand, and there are a multitude of career paths and advancement opportunities for workers who are skilled and certified in welding.

and great attention to detail and safety. A great variety of projects, such as tables, fire pits, coatracks, bookends, benches, jewelry holders, planters, signs, clocks, ramps, stoves, sculptures, garden art, gates, candleholders, picture frames, lamps, and virtually any other metal objects that can be envisioned, can be created with the welding equipment in a makerspace.

With abundant working space, a variety of tools and equipment, and infinite opportunities for learning and creating, makerspaces have quickly gained popularity as groundbreaking, hands-on learning hubs.

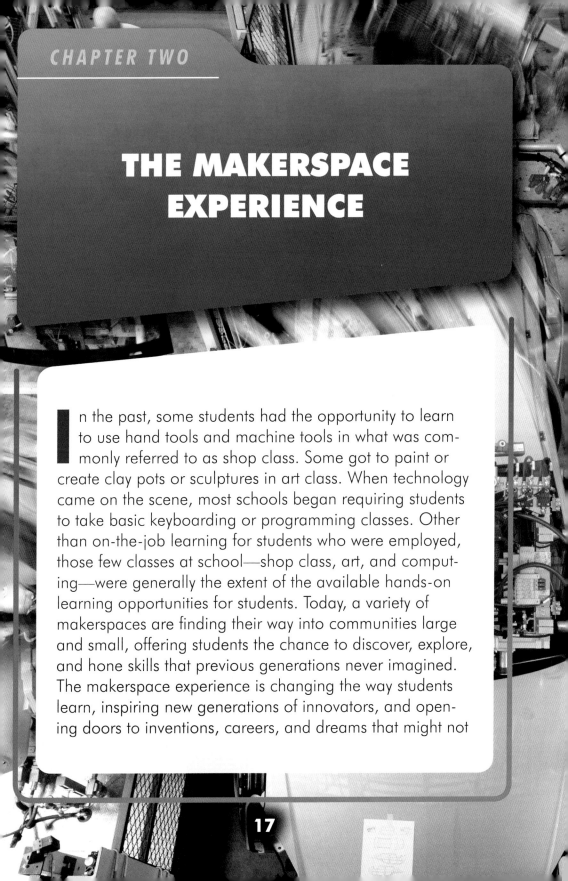

CHAPTER TWO

THE MAKERSPACE EXPERIENCE

In the past, some students had the opportunity to learn to use hand tools and machine tools in what was commonly referred to as shop class. Some got to paint or create clay pots or sculptures in art class. When technology came on the scene, most schools began requiring students to take basic keyboarding or programming classes. Other than on-the-job learning for students who were employed, those few classes at school—shop class, art, and computing—were generally the extent of the available hands-on learning opportunities for students. Today, a variety of makerspaces are finding their way into communities large and small, offering students the chance to discover, explore, and hone skills that previous generations never imagined. The makerspace experience is changing the way students learn, inspiring new generations of innovators, and opening doors to inventions, careers, and dreams that might not

As more and more schools cut back on the number and variety of art classes offered, many students are turning to makerspaces for an opportunity to learn and create.

have been realized otherwise. Students who seek out and get involved in makerspaces will find themselves well equipped to successfully step into future careers in hands-on industries such as manufacturing.

FINDING A MAKERSPACE

As long-standing institutions known not only for promoting a love of reading but also for fostering community engagement, it's no surprise that many libraries across the United States have developed makerspaces for their members' use. Although a makerspace may not be feasible in every branch of every public library system, a quick online search using a city name and the keywords "library makerspace" is a good way to find a nearby makerspace facility in a public library. For obvious reasons, library makerspaces do not include large, heavy industrial machines and equipment. Instead, the usual tools and devices might include computer workstations, iPads, Kindles, 3D printers, laser cutters, vinyl cutters, sewing machines and textiles, whiteboards, arts and crafts supplies, blocks such as LEGOs, K'Nex, small robots and robot parts, hand tools, and even small CNC router machines for cutting and engraving. Library patrons have free use of these makerspaces, as well as any help they might need from library staff to get started on their projects.

Privately funded makerspaces are becoming easier to find in urban areas. More of them are opening their doors all the time, thanks to a growing number of everyday makers—many of whom have longed to do more but simply didn't have access to the equipment they needed—and an enthusiastic response by communities as a whole. These urban makerspaces are typically large warehouse-type buildings that have the space to accommodate equipment for any and every type of maker. Typically, these spaces are funded by monthly or yearly membership fees. These fees help cover the cost of equipment and maintenance, property rental fees, insurance, and in some cases, wages for employees who keep the makerspace running and teach members how to use the equipment. Woodworking, automobile design and repair, all kinds of art, sewing, crafts, programming, machining, printing, and welding projects are all standard fare in these large makerspaces, most of which also have meeting rooms and group work spaces available to brainstorm and work together on projects.

According to a survey published by *Popular Science* magazine on February 23, 2016, there were fourteen times the number of makerspaces in use around the globe in 2016 than there were in 2006. In the United States, much of this growth has been and continues to be within schools. Increasingly, teachers and administrators have embraced the maker movement and incorporated making into their curricula, from kindergarten classrooms through grade

School makerspaces provide students with the resources they need to learn skills for a variety of careers, from manufacturing and engineering to fashion and design.

twelve. Some schools have established a makerspace within their library, supporting students of every grade level with tools and materials such as arts and crafts supplies, building supplies, computer labs, 3D printers, programming software, recording equipment, circuit boards, and building kits for robotics projects. In other schools, the students depend on their individual teachers for a makerspace area and experience, which varies depending on the space, supplies, and time each teacher has available. At the high school level, in many cases, makerspace labs have replaced what used to be a school's vocational classroom or workshop. At the collegiate level, makerspaces are being used to meet a wide range of needs, such as offering students the space and collaborative "think tank" environment they need to complete class projects or pursue individual goals, such as creating prototypes and launching their own start-ups. These makerspaces are usually equipped with a variety of both low- and high-tech equipment and have the added bonus of being housed in institutions of learning where students can turn to each other as well as knowledgeable experts in business, marketing, finance, the arts, technology, and virtually every type of industry for insight and inspiration.

MAKER FAIRES: A CELEBRATION OF MAKERS

Imagine a festive atmosphere and hundreds of makers—and all of their skills, crafts, products, devices, and creations—on display side by side. All of this, along with

STUDENTS MAKING A DIFFERENCE IN A MAKERSPACE

In 2017, Arkansas resident Patsy Smith was caring for a one-footed Indian Runner duck named Peg. She suspected Peg's missing foot had been bitten off by a turtle shortly after he hatched. He couldn't run or swim normally, and as he had grown, his leg had become more and more irritated and inflamed. Smith reached out with a Facebook post, hoping to find a prosthetic foot for Peg. At nearby Armorel High School, three eighth-grade students who were taking part in an innovative, tech-centric makerspace program led by teacher Alicia Bell saw Smith's post and answered the call. As part of their program, the students—Abby Simmons, Matthew Cook, and Darshan Patel—were learning to use a variety of software programs and 3D printers. The students used the equipment to manufacture a prosthetic foot for Peg. Many adjustments had to be made to account for the way Indian Runner ducks bend their knees and the way that Peg had learned to shift his weight as he tried to walk on his damaged leg. In all, it took more than thirty tries for the students to create the perfect prosthetic foot for Peg. Each try took more than three hours to print, and the students stayed after school for months and worked over their holiday break to complete the project. The final product was a prosthetic foot that allowed Peg the duck to stand, walk, and run like other ducks. This wasn't the first successful project undertaken by students in the program, and it wouldn't be the last. Previously, students had helped a classmate by designing and printing a special shoe insert, and soon after getting Peg up on two feet again, their teacher reported they were already hard at work on another prosthetic leg—this time for a local chicken!

plenty of food vendors, fun, interactive family activities, and big crowds of people, is what those who attend a Maker Faire get to experience. Dale Dougherty, father of the maker movement and chief executive officer (CEO) of Maker Media, held the first Maker Faire in San Mateo, California, in 2006 as a celebration of making and a chance for aspiring makers to participate in hands-on activities, learn new skills, and get a look at cutting-edge forms of art, technology, manufacturing, engineering, and experimentation. That first Maker Faire event drew a crowd of twenty thousand people, ensuring there would be more Maker Faires to come. The following year, two Maker Faires were held, one in the San Francisco Bay Area and one in Austin, Texas. By 2013, the maker movement was well underway, with 130 Maker Faires around the globe. In just four years, that number had grown to more than 240 Maker Faire events around the world. In 2014, the White House was host to a Maker Faire, with President Barack Obama lending his voice and support to the maker movement.

"New tools and technologies are making the building of things easier than ever," said Obama. "Across our country, ordinary Americans are inventing incredible things, and then they're able to bring them to these fairs. And you never know where this kind of enthusiasm and creativity and innovation could lead."

Many US cities have begun holding smaller-scale local events called Mini Faires. As these smaller faires grow in popularity and attendance, they often lead to the city hosting full-scale Maker Faires. Planning and organization is largely done by volunteers, with event planners putting out a call for makers of all types to participate. At any given

Maker Faires offer even the youngest attendees an opportunity to immerse themselves in a creative maker experience.

Mini or Maker Faire, attendees will have opportunities to engage with gardeners, artisans, programmers, performers, cooks, musicians, welders, mechanics, and designers of all types. In a relatively short amount of time, several of these events have grown to become highly anticipated annual events. The annual World Maker Faire New York and the Maker Faire Bay Area are known as the two flagship events for the maker movement, hosting a combined two-thousand-plus maker entries and more than two hundred thousand attendees each year!

CHAPTER THREE

MAKERSPACES AND MANUFACTURING

By fueling creativity and curiosity, promoting active creation and innovation, and providing the space, tools, and equipment for virtually any project, makerspaces are playing a significant role in classrooms and better equipping students for their future roles in the workforce. Virtually every industry stands to benefit as new generations of makers embark on careers, but the hands-on, collaborative, empowering environment of makerspaces promotes higher-order problem-solving skills that are especially prized in the manufacturing industry. The exposure to new skills, technologies, and machines that students gain in makerspaces can build a strong foundation for those looking forward to a rewarding career in manufacturing.

Makerspaces are paving the way for students interested in one of the many career paths in the manufacturing industry.

LEARNING MANUFACTURING
SKILLS IN MAKERSPACES

In manufacturing, it's crucial to handle any problems that arise quickly and efficiently to keep the production chain up and running and to prevent costly and inconvenient delays. Troubleshooting and problem solving are typically done on the workroom floor, as situations arise, rather than in scheduled boardroom meetings. This type of "on-the-fly" problem solving is common practice in makerspaces since makers encounter complications and setbacks with each project they take on or problem they set out to solve. Unlike traditional classroom learning, makerspace projects and problems aren't prearranged, and there's no answer key. When students at All Saints Episcopal School in Tyler, Texas, set out to manufacture a prosthetic arm for a twenty-two-year-old man in Honduras, their problem-solving skills were put to the test. They needed to create a prosthetic with precise specifications that would match up with the man's existing limb. The material needed to be somewhat flexible yet strong enough to withstand the heat generated in the manufacturing process. As challenges cropped up along the way, the students had to work through each one. These same problem-solving skills are used every day in manufacturing, and with each new challenge lies the potential to craft a solution that not only fixes the problem at hand, but also prevents similar problems from reoccurring in the workplace.

Responsibilities and day-to-day tasks in the manufacturing industry vary according to job specifications, but everyone successfully employed in the field relies on his or her ability to collaborate effectively with coworkers. Such collaboration is inherent in makerspaces, with makers often turning to one another to talk about their projects, work through issues, and receive vital constructive criticism on their processes and products. Manufacturing is not an insular pursuit; rather, it is an industry that—just as in makerspaces—embraces the collective brainpower and ingenuity of everyone on-site to achieve the highest level of efficiency and achievement.

MANUFACTURING JOBS: A MAKERSPACE BOOT CAMP SUCCESS STORY

In Baltimore, Maryland, a makerspace called the Foundery—equipped with the latest in heavy-duty and high-tech tools—is the site of a brand-new type of boot camp. As CEO of sports and apparel giant Under Armour and founder of a Baltimore-area real estate company, local businessperson Kevin Plank made a commitment to help grow the local workforce in exchange for support of his plans to develop the South Baltimore Peninsula. The idea was to recruit participants to take a series of classes at the Foundery over a six-week period. The Center for Urban Families refers participants, who so far have been men who enjoy working with their hands and are seeking work but have faced barriers in finding employment. Participants take classes four days a week and are paid fifteen dollars an hour while enrolled in the program. At the end of the six-week session, participants take part in a graduation ceremony, after which representatives from local manufacturing companies pass out business cards and look for new hires. The first eight participants in the makerspace boot camp graduated in January 2017. All of them received job offers upon graduation. Given the success of the first manufacturing boot camp, it's no surprise that the next class of recruits—double the size of the first—was anxious to begin boot camp immediately after the graduation ceremony!

In the heart of every maker is a yearning not only to make but to innovate. To create something new, something original that fills a void or serves a need is the end goal of most makers when they begin a project. Critical-thinking skills employed in makerspaces, such as logic and reasoning, are crucial to success in manufacturing and in any other industry that relies on a knowledgeable, innovative workforce. Innovators support growth in industries by consistently thinking outside and beyond the box to develop new products, procedures, and ideas.

EDUCATIONAL OPPORTUNITIES IN MANUFACTURING

While participation in makerspaces is proving to be an excellent stepping stone for students who wish to pursue a manufacturing career, it is by no means the only educational opportunity for such advancement. Youth apprenticeship programs, such as the one offered by the Aerospace Joint Apprenticeship Committee (AJAC) in Washington, provide a unique and challenging alternative for high school juniors and seniors. Through AJAC's Production Technician Youth Apprenticeship, students amass two thousand hours of skills that are directly applicable to the aerospace and advanced manufacturing industries. The program consists of a combination of class-room instruction hours and paid on-the-job training. AJAC partners with advanced manufacturing facilities where students work as production technicians, setting up, test-ing, and adjusting advanced manufacturing equipment while fulfilling their supervised, paid training hours. The

By taking advantage of resources such as makerspaces and vocational training, students give themselves a distinct advantage when it's time to embark on a career.

classroom instruction hours take place one day per week and may be completed at a partnering high school, a technical college, or a machine shop or makerspace. Upon

Many employers in the manufacturing industry offer apprenticeship programs, enabling them to teach job-specific skills to new recruits.

completion of the program, students have earned some money, gained valuable career skills, received high school credit toward graduation, earned fifteen hours of tuition-free college credits, and made some key contacts in the industry. There are similar programs in many states, and high school counselors or vocational teachers are great resources for learning what is available in a particular area.

Career and technical education (CTE) programs are another way for high school students to gain experience that is pertinent to manufacturing. Sometimes referred to as vocational or shop classes and programs, CTE offers hands-on classes, such as machine technology, engineering, woodworking, welding, and programming. Students learn how to use the latest technology, hand tools, machine tools, and CNC programs—as well as soft skills such as communication, critical thinking, time management, flexibility, teamwork, decision making, and conflict resolution—while completing projects together. Unfortunately, in recent years many school districts have cut funding for CTE programs, instead focusing solely on college preparedness for their students. According to the Bureau of Labor Statistics (BLS), 30 percent of high school graduates in 2016 did not enroll in college, and of the 70 percent of graduates who do enroll in college, nearly 40 percent do not complete the four-year programs they begin. Many argue that the decline in number of CTE programs has led to a shortage of skilled workers in the manufacturing industry and too many high school graduates facing very limited career options. As the makerspace movement gains momentum, it's helping to fill that void, but for high school students who still have the opportunity, taking part in a CTE program is an excellent way to gain the skills needed in the manufacturing industry.

When a CTE or apprenticeship program isn't a viable option, there is still a tried-and-true method for high school students to gain valuable job skills in a specific field. Many students seek part-time employment at a company that is in their desired industry. Manufacturing is required for all kinds of products at many different levels and in a variety of settings, so the odds of finding a company at which one can gain some entry-level manufacturing knowledge and skills is good. Finding a part-time job in manufacturing without gaining any skills beforehand might seem daunting, but motivation and a desire to learn can go a long way in an employer's eye, and often school counselors are more than happy to help match students with local employers.

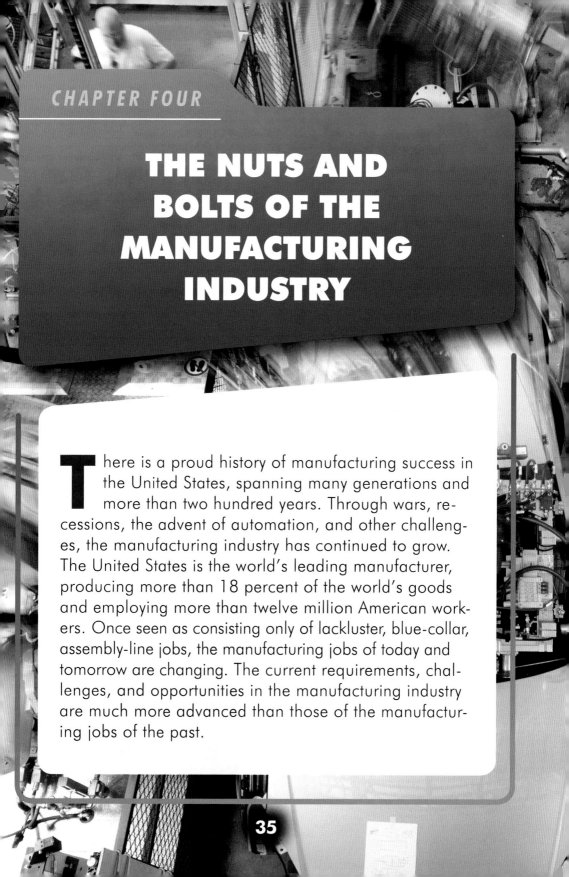

CHAPTER FOUR

THE NUTS AND BOLTS OF THE MANUFACTURING INDUSTRY

There is a proud history of manufacturing success in the United States, spanning many generations and more than two hundred years. Through wars, recessions, the advent of automation, and other challenges, the manufacturing industry has continued to grow. The United States is the world's leading manufacturer, producing more than 18 percent of the world's goods and employing more than twelve million American workers. Once seen as consisting only of lackluster, blue-collar, assembly-line jobs, the manufacturing jobs of today and tomorrow are changing. The current requirements, challenges, and opportunities in the manufacturing industry are much more advanced than those of the manufacturing jobs of the past.

Beginning with Henry Ford's assembly line for his Model T, the US automobile industry revolutionized the mass production assembly line.

THE HISTORY OF US MANUFACTURING

Samuel Slater is widely regarded as the father of the American Industrial Revolution. Relying on what he had learned in early British mills, Slater opened the first industrial cotton mill in the United States in 1790. This marked the beginning of the Industrial Revolution in America and the beginning of a transformation in the workforce. Prior to this time, the economy was largely driven by agriculture. Slater's industrial cotton mill paved the way for other mills, factories, and machines that enabled manufacturing of goods to take place on a grand scale.

In 1798, cotton gin inventor Eli Whitney struck on the brilliant idea of manufacturing guns using interchangeable parts. Soon, many other businesses were incorporating Whitney's idea into their own manufacturing processes. Another milestone in manufacturing history was the invention of a high-pressure steam engine by Oliver Evans in 1804. The engine was adapted for use in many different industries, and within a few short years it propelled ships across oceans and was used to operate mills and factories for manufacturing everything from flour to textiles.

As America flourished and the workforce grew exponentially due to millions of immigrants seeking a better life, the manufacturing industry continued to advance at an astounding rate. Machine tools were perfected, and strategies for streamlining and improving the manufacturing process began to take shape.

In the late 1890s, industrial engineers began taking a closer look at factors affecting the efficiency and end products at factories. Frank and Lillian Gilbreth were the early industrial engineers credited with inventing process charts. These are charts that look at all elements that affect the manufacturing process, including things like the motivations and attitudes of workers. Frederick W. Taylor studied workers and their individual work methods, using science to come up with the concept of standardized work. Standardized work is a construct still used today and involves determining the rate at which products need to be made,

LEAN MANUFACTURING AND THE EIGHT WASTES

The success or failure of a manufacturer is determined to a great extent by the overall efficiency of its production practices. The *Business Dictionary* provides this definition for "lean manufacturing":

Doing more with less by employing "lean thinking." Lean manufacturing involves never ending efforts to eliminate or reduce "muda" (Japanese for waste or any activity that consumes resources without adding value) in design, manufacturing, distribution, and customer service processes.

The eight wastes of lean manufacturing include the following:

1. Defects: When end products are not fit for use.
2. Excess processing: When end products must be repaired or reworked to meet the customer's needs.
3. Overproduction: When more end products are produced than customers are willing to purchase.
4. Waiting: When there is inaction or lag time during a product's processing.
5. Inventory: When products are complete but are being stored because they have not yet been sold.
6. Moving: When products are transported, during which there is additional cost and no value added.
7. Motion: When value is not being added to a product because of unnecessary motion due to things like inefficient shop floor layouts or improper equipment.
8. Nonutilized talent: When all employees' talents are not being utilized and efforts are being wasted on menial tasks instead.

the specific sequence of work tasks and movements required, and the types and number of machines and equipment required to maintain the production rate.

In 1910, Henry Ford and his business partner, Charles E. Sorensen, took things a step further. They developed the first comprehensive manufacturing strategy, which Ford used—with great success—in his factory for manufacturing the Model T automobile. Later, when Ford's factories were used for war production during World War II, his manufacturing strategy proved very effective and played a key role in the Allied victory. After the war, the success of American pioneers of the manufacturing industry was studied closely by industrialists in Japan. Executives at Toyota Motor Company expanded on manufacturing practices utilized by Ford and others in America. Based on their studies of American manufacturing, the Japanese executives developed an approach called just-in-time production. Over the years, manufacturers continued to build on this successful approach. There were many similar models proposed under different names, but they were all essentially just-in-time production. One phrase—lean manufacturing—finally stuck and is widely practiced in successful manufacturing operations around the world today.

AN EVOLVING INDUSTRY: CHANGES AND CHALLENGES IN MANUFACTURING

There's no denying that some types of manufacturing jobs are dwindling in America. Some manufacturing companies have chosen to set up shop in other countries, such as Mexico and China, where they can pay workers lower wages and therefore make bigger profits. These jobs are typically fairly unskilled manufacturing positions, involving manual tasks that don't require any advanced coursework or training to complete. Many manufacturing positions have also been lost to automation since simple, repetitive work once performed by people on the workroom floor is able to be done by the more advanced machines of today. Some types of manufacturing are growing, however. The demand for employees in advanced manufacturing positions is growing, and for those who are qualified to fill the positions, the outlook is very bright. Advanced manufacturing jobs generally offer good benefits, job stability, and

The advantages of working in the manufacturing industry include higher than average wages and a challenging work environment that encourages innovation and teamwork.

much higher salaries than the manufacturing jobs of days past. As expected, though, to be successful in landing these specialized positions, most applicants will need to have completed college-level coursework. High school CTE programs and apprenticeships are a great place to start, but a bachelor's degree in manufacturing or a related field can open many more doors. For those drawn to the creative side of manufacturing as well as the technical aspects, an advanced degree in engineering can lead to a career as a design engineer. There are also courses and certifications in highly specialized areas, such as welding, quality control, and computer-aided design (CAD), that some manufacturing positions require. Upper-level management and engineering positions often require a master's degree in manufacturing processes or engineering. There is also

A CAREER IN MANUFACTURING: Q & A WITH ERIC HICKS

Eric Hicks is a quality engineer at CFAN, a manufacturer of composite fan blades for large aircraft engines. Hicks has also worked as a technician, a manufacturing engineer, and a production business leader. In the following interview with the author, Hicks offers some great insights for students considering a career in manufacturing.

What are some of the most interesting aspects of your job?

I really enjoy the troubleshooting/problem solving aspects of my job. I enjoy data analysis using statistics to show why we may have an issue related to specific variables. I also enjoy getting away from my computer and performing experiments on the shop floor.

Was a four-year degree required for your career in manufacturing?

In a previous position in semiconductor manufacturing, I earned a two-year associate's degree and worked as a technician on equipment. In my current aerospace manufacturing career, a four-year degree is essential. The advantage of a four-year degree is the ability to move into more advanced positions, including supervisory and technical paths, as well as income growth potential.

Are there any specific classes or experiences students can take part in to prepare for a career in manufacturing?

Looking back, learning to type quickly and efficiently has been a huge help in my job. Math and science classes definitely help you to solve problems in a methodical, data-driven method. Organizational and computer skills including software such as PowerPoint, Excel, etc. are also very valuable. Makerspaces appear to be great programs. I've had similar types of experiences and they really help challenge your mind.

Is the industry currently in a state of growth?

The industry is absolutely growing, but we have to be flexible and mindful of the changing environment of automation and cost reduction. Manufacturing is a great opportunity for anyone with interest in how things are made and how they work.

the option of completing a two-year associate's degree program in engineering or manufacturing technology. Academic requirements will vary, depending on the specific position, the level of demand, and the employer, but the most promising manufacturing jobs of the future will all require training and education beyond high school.

OUTLOOK FOR THE MANUFACTURING INDUSTRY

According to a 2016 report by the White House Subcommittee on Advanced Manufacturing, 3.5 million advanced manufacturing positions will need to be filled between 2016 and 2026. Companies that manufacture highly specialized parts or equipment—such as Micropulse in Columbia City, Indiana, which manufactures specialized medical equipment—are experiencing rapid growth. "There's always going to be a certain amount of

Pursuing a career in manufacturing is a good plan because jobs are consistently available and will likely be far into the future.

jobs you can't automate away," says Micropulse CEO Brian Emerick. Micropulse went from 190 employees in 2012 to 306 in 2017—a prime example of the trend toward growth and higher demand in advanced manufacturing facilities. Manufacturing jobs fall into several different categories, as defined by the BLS. Between 2016 and 2026, the BLS estimates there will be only a 1 percent growth rate in machinist and tool and die maker jobs, describing these positions as having little or no change. Manufacturing jobs the BLS predicts will have a healthy growth rate between 2016 and 2026 include boilermakers, with 9 percent growth, industrial machinery maintenance workers, with 7 percent, and welders, with 6 percent. The BLS predicts 25,100 jobs for industrial engineers will open up between 2016 and 2026, which is a faster-than-average 10 percent growth rate. Unskilled manufacturing positions such as hand laborers and material movers will see a 7 percent growth rate, while assemblers will see a 14 percent decline in jobs, which will mean a loss of 261,900 jobs between 2016 and 2026. Given these estimates, it's clear that the manufacturing positions that are most secure are those that are more specialized and require a postsecondary education.

CHAPTER FIVE

TYPES OF
MANUFACTURING JOBS

T he manufacturing industry is a giant. It encompasses a wide variety of career options, job settings, skill sets, and areas of specialization. Despite the many variables within the field, there are common traits and abilities that are helpful in every type of manufacturing position. These include critical-thinking skills, the ability to work well with others, an interest in making, and proficiency in problem solving. All of these skills are honed in programs such as CTE and apprenticeships and through participation in makerspaces, and all are essential to acquiring a prosperous manufacturing career, no matter the job title.

PRODUCTION WORKERS

Production workers make up the largest sector of manufacturing, with more employees than any other area. This is also

With advances in robotics and an increasing number of machines that can perform human tasks, automation is changing the face of the manufacturing industry.

the sector of manufacturing poised to take the largest hit over the next decade, with many production-worker positions in the United States being lost to automation and outsourcing to other countries. These jobs are often performed in an assembly line and typically involve repetitive tasks. Depending on the type of product being manufactured, production workers may also work in individual workstations. These positions usually do not require a postsecondary degree, and any special training required is done on the job. Production workers are used in many different types of manufacturing industries, from auto parts to textiles to the food and beverage industry.

Technicians play an important role in the manufacturing industry. The type of technicians employed by a manufacturing company varies

WINNING WORKPLACES IN MANUFACTURING

The manufacturing industry is immense, employing more than twelve million people in the United States and providing jobs in a variety of specialty areas. Though location may be a determining factor when job seekers choose where to apply, finding a company that is known for providing its employees with a great work environment and overall job satisfaction is important. For those who are open to relocating for the right job, thoroughly researching top employers and targeting those that have

Earning a livable wage is crucial, but other important considerations in a job search include finding an employer who is communicative and open to new ideas.

the most to offer can mean the difference between feeling just OK about a job and really enjoying a career. In 2018, *Fortune* published the results of a survey of thousands of employees conducted by Great Places to Work. Participants were asked about things such as work atmosphere, challenges, management style, their sense of pride in their workplace, and rewards. Here are the top twenty workplaces in manufacturing in the United States and their locations:

- Stryker Corporation in Kalamazoo, Michigan
- JM Family Enterprises Inc. in Deerfield Beach, Florida
- FONA International Inc. in Geneva, Illinois
- Mars Inc. in McLean, Virginia
- American Transmission Company in Waukesha, Wisconsin
- Hilcorp in Houston, Texas
- Concho Resources in Midland, Texas
- FOH Inc. in Miami, Florida
- Devon Energy in Oklahoma City, Oklahoma
- Graco Inc. in Minneapolis, Minnesota
- Arthrex Inc. in Naples, Florida
- Pro Food Systems Inc. in Holts Summit, Missouri
- Connectrac in Dallas, Texas
- Reynolds American Inc. in Winston-Salem, North Carolina
- Powerblanket in Salt Lake City, Utah
- Michelin North America in Greenville, South Carolina
- Radio Systems Corporation in Knoxville, Tennessee
- Niagara Conservation in Flower Mound, Texas
- Opus One Winery LLC in Oakville, California
- 3M Company in St. Paul, Minnesota

according to the products being manufactured. Most manufacturing companies have calibration technicians on staff. Calibration technicians must have vast knowledge of the tools used to test and calibrate machines, such as oscilloscopes, pressure gauges, calipers, and temperature controllers. They are responsible for maintaining and repairing all machines and equipment used in a manufacturing facility. Most calibration technicians have an associate's degree in instrumentation or technology. Repair and maintenance technicians are on staff at all sizable manufacturing facilities. Their job responsibilities include performing tasks to maintain the overall functionality of the facility, including electrical, plumbing, alarm, and HVAC systems, as well as landscape maintenance. Repair and maintenance technicians must possess a broad skill set and have great attention to detail, but these positions do not necessarily require any formal training or postsecondary education. Quality-control technicians ensure quality and safety standards of the company are met. Their responsibilities include preventing and resolving issues pertaining to employee performance as well as product outcomes. Maintaining employee adherence to rules, safety guidelines, and required training is part of the job, as is finding solutions to any problems with the manufacturing process that are impacting the quality of products. Quality-control technicians may or may not have a postsecondary degree, but they are usually required to obtain certification from the American Society for Quality.

TOOL AND DIE MAKERS

Tool and die makers play a pivotal role in the day-to-day operations of manufacturing facilities. It's the job of tool and die makers to set up and operate a variety of CNC machines and other tools, such as lathes, milling machines, and grinders, in order to create the metal parts and tools that are used to produce products. These parts can include tool bits, jigs, gauges, milling cutters, and metal dies. Dies are like industrial cookie cutters. They are made from metal blocks and are used to cut or shape a variety of materials, such as metal, plastic, and even food, to create all kinds of products, from computer chips to pasta to automobile parts. Tool and die makers must be well versed in CAD programs. These programs are used to create blueprints for the products and tools to be produced. When the desired tool or die is completed, tool and die makers test them to make sure they meet exact specifications, and if they do not, the tool and die makers do any necessary alterations. Many tool and die makers are trained through apprenticeship programs or on-the-job training. They may or may not be required to have postsecondary education.

BOILERMAKERS

Boilers are large metal containers that heat water or other fluid to generate electric power and to provide heat. Boilermakers assemble, maintain, and repair boilers and large

Working as a boilermaker is physically demanding but does not require a college degree and provides an opportunity to travel as well as great earning potential.

tanks and vats that are used to store liquid chemicals, beverages, and other products. Tanks, vats, and boilers are found on ships, in factories, and in many types of buildings. Work as a boilermaker involves travel, sometimes far from home. The work is physically demanding, and the conditions are often dark, damp, and cramped. Boilermakers must know how to use a variety of hand and power tools, such as welders, torches, levels, wedges, and turnbuckles. Boilers can last for fifty years or more and must be regularly maintained and repaired throughout their life span. This is work that must be performed by a live person, so boilermakers are not in danger of being put out of business due to automation. Boilermakers acquire their skills from apprenticeships or on-the-job training and do not need a college degree.

ENGINEERS

There are many types of engineers. In manufacturing, design engineers perform a variety of functions. They may be called on to design new products to take to market or to design machinery and equipment to be used in the manufacture of products. They also make modifications to existing products to improve performance. Design engineers use CAD software programs to design their idea, and then create a prototype to bring their model to life. The prototype is tested, and if it functions as hoped, the design is then put into production. If changes are required, the design engineer goes back to the drawing board to make changes that will improve the design. Design engineers have completed a postsecondary degree program, usually in engineering. Logistics engineers are responsible for the transportation, storage, and delivery of goods. Though that sounds straightforward and simple, their job involves much more than storing and moving things. Logistics engineers use science, math, and tech skills to analyze data related to product storage and distribution. They identify any problematic issues and come up with solutions. They devise plans for improving existing storage, transportation, and delivery practices to better serve the manufacturing company and its customers. Logistics engineers have a strong background in math and science, and most have a four-year degree.

CHAPTER SIX

ESSENTIAL JOB-SEARCH SKILLS

There are many types of jobs within the manufacturing industry, and choosing just the right career path is an important decision. Whether the goal is to gain entry-level experience on the manufacturing floor or to earn an advanced degree and aim for a supervisory role right from the start, every first job begins with a basic job search. There are essential tools and skills that everyone needs to find promising job leads and to turn those leads into potential career opportunities. Once the academic requirements have been met and any necessary skills and experience attained, it's time to begin putting those tools and skills to good use as the job-search process begins. Drafting a winning résumé, keeping a positive attitude, making the most of job-search resources, and thoroughly preparing for interviews will pave the way to landing a great job in manufacturing.

A WINNING RÉSUMÉ

A résumé can be thought of as a written highlight reel of a person's finest academic and professional achievements, captured neatly and concisely on a page. Though the basic information conveyed and overall goal of all résumés may be the same, there are nearly as many styles of résumés as there are applicants. A great first step is to view a number of sample résumés online, especially those tailored for positions in the manufacturing industry or similar industries. With a preferred style in mind, a résumé can be drafted from scratch in a word processing program or one can be created with the help of premade résumé templates. There are many websites, such as Resume Genius and Hloom, that offer free résumé templates. Job seekers can choose the style of template

Job seekers will need to spend a good deal of time crafting a well-written, error-free résumé that will grab the attention of potential employers.

they prefer, download it, and simply enter their text. Other than hiring a professional résumé writer, however, there is really no shortcut when it comes to the text itself, so applicants need to be prepared to spend considerable time and effort on things like wording, grammar, and punctuation when drafting a résumé.

Résumés should begin with the applicant's name and contact information. This is often followed by a personal statement of career objective. The career objective statement should reassure the hiring manager of the skills, abilities, and traits the applicant possesses that will be an asset to the company. The career objective statement is not meant to be a statement of what the applicant would like to gain from working at the company. Following the career objective statement should be a list of relevant professional experience. For entry-level candidates, this may be limited to high school jobs or volunteer experiences, and that's OK. Everyone starts somewhere. The next section of the résumé lists education. Any special honors or awards achieved in school should be listed, as well as the name of the school, date of graduation, and GPA. Finally, any special skills, memberships, or certifications can be listed at the bottom of the résumé. Always have one or two reliable proofreaders with a sharp eye for detail read over the résumé before sending it out. Oftentimes, résumés are simply emailed, but when printing copies of a résumé, it's important to use high-quality paper that is thicker than the average printer paper.

Remember, each résumé has only seconds to make a first impression on the hiring manager. Here are a few quick tips to keep in mind while writing a résumé:

- Research all prospective employers and customize the career objective statement for each one.
- Rather than complete sentences, use bullet points that begin with action words to highlight your strengths and achievements.
- Be clear, specific, and to the point in describing your accomplishments.
- Show enthusiasm and confidence, but be careful not to cross the line into arrogance.
- Always double-check for typos, grammar, and spelling errors—and have others check as well!

THE JOB SEARCH: WHERE TO LOOK

Job seeking can be exhausting and sometimes even nerve-racking, but thankfully, it doesn't have to be expensive. There are a number of free, online resources to help match job seekers with companies looking to hire people with their skill set. The sites are set up similarly, but each features unique search tools. Some of the most user-friendly sites allow users to search according to location, employer, job skills, or job title. There are hundreds of job-search sites, and job seekers will want to choose several of them to use because every job listing won't appear on every job-search site. Popular job-search sites include Glassdoor, Monster, Indeed, LinkedIn, Google for Jobs, CareerBuilder, Dice, Idealist, and US.jobs. There are also some sites that are designed to let job seekers post their own specific requirements when it comes to the position they're seeking. These sites allow users to narrow down the listings

DRESSING FOR SUCCESS

Dressing to impress is the goal of every interviewee, but at the same time, no one wants to feel overdressed. Workplaces within the manufacturing industry typically have a fairly laid-back dress code, making many applicants unsure of whether they should go the extra mile and wear a suit to an interview for a manufacturing job. The quick answer is: it's never wrong to wear a suit. It shows attention to detail and gives the hiring manager the distinct impression that an applicant is motivated and professional. However, it is certainly not necessary to go to the expense of purchasing professional business

Making a great first impression is crucial, and applicants who make an effort to dress in appropriate business attire will stand out to a hiring manager.

attire for an interview in this field. A pair of khaki pants is a great option and can be paired with a belt and dress shoes for a polished look. T-shirts should never be worn to an interview. All clothes should be clean and wrinkle free, and care should be taken to present an overall clean and pleasant appearance. Experience, skill, motivation, and attitude are certainly the most important qualities in any candidate, but dressing appropriately for an interview is a step that can't be skipped when trying to land a job in manufacturing.

and avoid unwanted contact about jobs that don't fit their requirements.

Job fairs are also excellent opportunities for job seekers and often are industry specific. Those interested in a manufacturing job could attend a job fair for manufacturing industry positions and have the chance to learn about openings at many different companies all in one day. Attendees often have the opportunity to speak with hiring managers at the event and can submit applications and résumés to the companies they feel are the best fit. Job fairs sometimes include on-the-spot interviews, so it's a good idea for attendees to come prepared and to dress as if they are going to an interview.

Social media platforms, such as LinkedIn, Facebook, and Twitter, can be effective tools to use while job searching, both for networking with others who might know of a job lead and as a way to learn more about companies and organizations that are of interest. Job seekers should make sure their personal, online presence doesn't include anything that would be a red flag for employers. It's commonplace for employers to research applicants, and an unflattering, irresponsible, or thoughtless post on the internet may be enough to keep a hiring manager from extending an invitation to interview.

ACING THE INTERVIEW

With a polished résumé in hand and a well-researched list of companies to send it to, the final hurdle in the job search is acing the interview. It can be very helpful to search for and watch mock interviews online, especially for entry-level candidates without much interview experience. Every interview will most likely include a few questions that are unique to the specific position, company, or hiring manager conducting the interview, but there are some commonly asked interview questions that are important to review. Some of the most common interview questions include the following:

- How did you hear about this job?
- What do you know about this company?
- Can you tell me a little about yourself?
- Why do you feel you're a good fit for our company?
- What are your greatest professional strengths/ weaknesses?
- Can you tell me about a conflict you've faced at work and how you handled it?

After giving careful consideration to these questions, the final step in preparing for an interview is to hold a practice interview, with help from a friend or family member. To achieve the most benefit from this exercise, the person playing the role of hiring manager should be prepared to vary the questions each time and to give constructive feedback, and the interviewee should dress and behave as if it were a real interview.

When it's time for the real interview, applicants should arrive at least five minutes early, remain calm and relaxed, use positive body language, such as smiling and making eye contact, and fully engage in the interview, both answering and asking questions. Applicants who are well prepared, friendly, sincere, and project confidence without sounding rehearsed will tip the scales in favor of a

Job applicants should practice ahead of time and be prepared to take part in a group interview as well as a one-on-one interview.

successful interview that ends in a job offer. After the interview, it's a professional courtesy and a nice personal touch to reach out to the hiring manager to thank him or her. This gesture shows that an applicant is appreciative of the manager's time, enthusiastic about the company and the opportunity, and thoughtful. An email or a note expressing thanks are both an acceptable way to follow up. This can also be viewed as one final opportunity for applicants to stand out to a hiring manager who might have interviewed dozens of applicants.

Though there are many changes happening, and some jobs within the industry are dwindling, overall, the manufacturing industry has much to offer those who have an interest in the production of goods. Now more than ever, as positions in manufacturing are becoming increasingly advanced and specialized, hands-on learning opportunities, such as those presented in makerspaces, CTE programs, and apprenticeships, are beneficial. Pursuing advanced training or a college degree in manufacturing or a related field is advantageous for those who would like to work in a skilled position in manufacturing. There are entry-level positions for high school graduates that provide on-the-job training, but those who are willing to complete additional training and education hours beyond high school will have the best chance of enjoying a stable, rewarding, long-term career in manufacturing.

GLOSSARY

apprenticeship A program in which one works for an expert in a field to gain knowledge and experience.

automation The use of advanced technology to run machines and equipment.

collaboration The act of working together with others.

dongle An electronic device that, when attached to a computer, enables a specific function.

efficiency The quality of avoiding any wasted time or effort.

evolving Changing and advancing over time.

insular Isolated or alone.

logistics The management of all aspects of supply and delivery of products or services.

momentum A force or strength that moves something along.

outsourcing The practice of using a labor force or supplier outside of the immediate area or region.

pivotal Very important; crucial.

proficiency Having great skill in something.

prosperous Positive or profitable circumstances.

prosthetic A replacement part for the body.

prototype An example or model.

recession A period when the economy takes a turn for the worse and there are hard times financially.

repetitive Describing something that happens over and over again, in the same way.

résumé A written summary of academic and work experience.

stymied Hindered in the completion of something.

template A model or basic outline of something that can be customized by the user.

textiles Products made with fabric, such as clothing.

viable Possible; able to be done, given the circumstances.

Futuremakers
120 W. North Avenue
Baltimore, MD 21201
(202) 683-8609
Website: http://www.kidsmakethingsbetter.com
Facebook and Instagram: @futuremakerkids
Futuremakers offers a mobile makerspace experience for
    students. Its website includes information about pop-up
    makerspace labs and creative workshop opportunities
    for those interested in makerspace lab experiences.

Maker Education Initiative
1001 Forty-Second Street, Suite 230
Oakland, CA 94608
(510) 655-1935
Website: http://makered.org
Facebook: @MakerEducationInitiative
Twitter: @MakerEdOrg
The Maker Education Initiative is a nonprofit organization
    that supports educators of youth makers. Its web-
    site includes a list of training and resources for those
    interested in makerspace learning opportunities. Also
    included are video links to tours of makerspaces,
    schools, libraries, and museums to inspire and assist
    others in putting together their own makerspace.

National Association of Manufacturers (NAM)
733 Tenth Street NW, Suite 700
Washington, DC 20001

(800) 814-8468
Website: http://www.nam.org
Facebook: @NAMpage
Twitter: @shopfloornam
The NAM is a leading advocate of the manufacturing
    industry in the United States, providing support and
    up-to-date information on key issues. Its website offers
    in-depth information about NAM membership, educa-
    tion, careers, and economic data and reports related to
    the field of manufacturing.

Nation of Makers
110 University Boulevard, #752
Silver Spring, MD 20918
Website: http://nationofmakers.us
Facebook: @nationofmakers
Twitter: @NationOfMakers
The Nation of Makers supports prospective makers and the
    nationwide maker community. Its website offers educa-
    tional and financial resources for makers, as well as an
    extensive list of businesses and organizations advocating
    for the maker movement.

Nuts, Bolts & Thingamajigs
2135 Point Boulevard
Elgin, IL 60123
(815) 399-8700
Website: https://www.nutsandboltsfoundation.org
Facebook: @nutsandboltsfoundation
Twitter: @NBThingamajigs
Nuts, Bolts & Thingamajigs strives to inspire and support

future generations of makers, inventors, and manufacturers. Its website provides information about scholarships and camps the organization offers, as well as an extensive list of student resources for those interested in learning more about a career in manufacturing.

Site 3 coLaboratory
718R Ossington Avenue
Toronto, ON M6G 2T7
Canada
Website: http://www.site3.ca
Facebook and Twitter: @site3colab
Site 3 coLaboratory is a Toronto-based arts and tech makerspace venue. Its website lists space and equipment availability, open house dates, and other educational maker events and offerings.

SkullSpace
374 Donald Street, 2nd Floor
Winnipeg, MB R3B 2J2
Canada
(204) 480-4092
Website: https://skullspace.ca
Facebook: @SkullSpaceWpg
Twitter: @skullspacewpg
SkullSpace is a Canadian organization that offers membership and access to a large makerspace facility. Its website includes a detailed description of the space and equipment available to members, as well as a complete list of upcoming events and presentations.

Society of Manufacturing Engineers (SME) Education Foundation

1000 Town Center, Suite 1910
Southfield, MI 48075
(313) 425-3300
Website: https://www.smeef.org
Facebook: @SME.Education.Foundation
Twitter: @mfgeducation
The SME Education Foundation is dedicated to promoting awareness of emerging opportunities in the manufacturing industry and offering educational options for students who are interested in a future career in manufacturing. Its website offers information about the organization's history, available scholarships, success stories, and the latest information about the manufacturing industry.

FOR FURTHER READING

Branwyn, Gareth. *Make: Tips and Tales from the Workshop*. San Francisco, CA: Maker Media, 2018.

Burker, Josh. *The Invent to Learn Guide to Fun: Makerspace, Classroom, Library, and Home STEM Projects*. Torrance, CA: Constructing Modern Knowledge Press, 2015.

Challoner, Jack. *Maker Lab: 28 Super Cool Projects: Build * Invent * Create * Discover*. New York, NY: DK Children, 2016.

Craig, Joe. *The Vo-Tech Track to Success in Manufacturing, Mechanics, and Automotive Care*. New York, NY: Rosen Publishing, 2015.

Davies, Sarah R. *Hackerspaces: Making the Maker Movement*. Malden, MA: Polity Press, 2017.

Dougherty, Dale, and Ariane Conrad. *Free to Make*. Berkeley, CA: North Atlantic Books, 2016.

Fleming, Laura. *The Kickstart Guide to Making GREAT Makerspaces*. Thousand Oaks, CA: Corwin, 2017.

Hatch, Mark. *The Maker Movement Manifesto*. New York, NY: McGraw-Hill Education, 2013.

Martin, Danielle, and Alisha Panjwani. *Start Making! A Guide to Engaging Young People in Maker Activities*. San Francisco, CA: Maker Media, 2016.

Morganelli, Adrianna. *Dream Jobs in Manufacturing*. New York, NY: Crabtree Publishing, 2018.

Sack, Rebekah. *The Young Adult's Survival Guide to Interviews: Finding the Job and Nailing the Interview*. Ocala, FL: Atlantic Publishing Group, 2016.

Terranova, Andrew, and Sharon Rose. *How Things Are Made*. New York, NY: Black Dog & Leventhal, 2018.

BIBLIOGRAPHY

Amadeo, Kimberly. "Want to Earn $82,023 a Year? Get One of These Jobs." Balance, July 31, 2018. https://www.thebalance.com/manufacturing-jobs-examples-types-and-changes-3305941.

Babcock, Stephen. "This Makerspace Is Bringing the Bootcamp Concept to Manufacturing." Technical.ly Baltimore, March 20, 2017. https://technical.ly/baltimore/2017/03/20/foundery-sagamore-manufacturing-bootcamp.

Barksdale, Savanna. "Students Use Self-Directed Learning to Serve Their Community, One Foot at a Time." *Homeroom* (blog), US Department of Education, March 16, 2018. https://blog.ed.gov/2018/03/students-use-self-directed-learning-to-serve-their-community-one-foot-at-a-time.

Bentley, Kipp. "Makerspaces: New Prospects for Hands-On Learning in Schools." Center for Digital Education, February 12, 2017. http://www.govtech.com/education/news/makerspaces.html.

Bentley, Kipp. "A Rebirth for Career and Technical Education." Center for Digital Education, January 26, 2017. http://www.govtech.com/education/news/a-rebirth-for-career-and-technical-education.html.

Donahue, Michelle Z. "What Is a Maker Faire, Exactly?" *Smithsonian*, June 12, 2015. https://www.smithsonianmag.com/innovation/what-maker-faire-exactly-180955574.

Fallows, Deborah. "How Libraries Are Becoming Modern Makerspaces." *Atlantic*, March 17, 2016. https://www

.theatlantic.com/technology/archive/2016/03/everyone
-is-a-maker/473286.

Fortune. "The 20 Best Workplaces in Manufacturing and
Production." September 11, 2018. http://fortune
.com/2018/09/11/20-best-workplaces-manufacturing
-production-2018.

Henschen, Holly. "Use of Math, Creativity All Part of CNC
Machining." *Washington State Journal* (Ritzville, WA),
January 28, 2017. https://madison.com/wsj/business
/use-of-math-creativity-all-part-of-cnc-machining
/article_3931409c-55a5-5cc9-951c-0ea530105df0
.html.

Herzog, Rachel. "PHOTOS: Arkansas Students Print 3-D Leg
for Duck." *Arkansas Democrat-Gazette* (Little Rock, AR),
January 5, 2018. https://www.arkansasonline.com
/news/2018/jan/05/photo-arkansas-students-print-3
-d-leg-duck.

Hicks, Eric. "A Career in Manufacturing: Q & A with Eric
Hicks." Email interview, October 5, 2018.

Hitner, Mara. "How to Build a Successful Makerspace."
MatterHackers, August 22, 2017. https://www
.matterhackers.com/news/how-to-build-a-successful
-makerspace.

Lynch, Matthew. "Why Makerspaces Are the Key to Innovation." Tech Edvocate, February 21, 2017. https://www
.thetechedvocate.org/why-makerspaces-are-the-key
-to-innovation.

Makerspaces.com. "What Is a Makerspace? Is It a Hacker-
space or a Makerspace?" March 15, 2017. https://www
.makerspaces.com/what-is-a-makerspace.

Muirhead, Rob. "What Is CNC Machining?" Goodwin

College, June 27, 2018. https://www.goodwin.edu /enews/what-is-cnc.

Schmidt, Mike. "Manufacturing's Maker Movement Revolution." Association of Equipment Manufacturers, July 13, 2017. https://www.aem.org/news/july-2017 /manufacturings-maker-movement-revolution.

Semuels, Alana. "America Is Still Making Things." *Atlantic*, January 6, 2017. https://www .theatlantic.com/business/archive/2017/01 /america-is-still-making-things/512282.

Sherman, Natalie. "Port Covington Manufacturing Bootcamp Underway." *Baltimore (MD) Sun*, February 16, 2017. https://www.baltimoresun.com/news/maryland /baltimore-city/bs-bz-city-garage-manufacturing -bootcamp-20170216-story.html#.

Tierney, John. "How Makerspaces Help Local Economies." *Atlantic*, April 17, 2015. https://www .theatlantic.com/technology/archive/2015/04 /makerspaces-are-remaking-local-economies/390807.

Waters, John K. "What Makes a Great Makerspace?" *THE Journal*, October 20, 2016. https://thejournal.com /Articles/2016/10/20/What-Makes-a-Great -Makerspace.aspx?Page=1.

Weis, Dusty. "Incubators and Makerspaces Offer Manufacturers Untapped Talent Pool." Association of Equipment Manufacturers, May 31, 2018. https://www.aem.org /news/incubators-and-makerspaces-offer -manufacturers-untapped-talent-pool.

Wilkinson, Karen. "Makers Wanted." *Comstock's*, April 3, 2018. https://www.comstocksmag.com/longreads /makers-wanted.

INDEX

A

advanced degrees, 42, 57
Aerospace Joint Apprenticeship Committee (AJAC), 30–31
apprenticeship, 30–31, 34, 42, 47, 53, 55, 66
artwork, 4, 6, 9–10
associate's degree, 42, 43, 44, 52
automation, 35, 40, 43, 44, 46, 47, 49, 55
automotive and assembly work, 7, 13–14

B

bachelor's degree, 42, 66
boilermakers, 46, 53, 55
boot camp, makerspace, 29
Bureau of Labor Statistics (BLS), 33–34
   estimates, 46

C

career and technical education (CTE) program, 33, 34, 42, 47, 66
classes
   art, 17
   college, 22
   CTE, 33

Foundery, 29
   in makerspaces, 7
   math and science, 43
   programming, 17
   shop, 17, 33
CNC machines, 6, 53
   milling machines, 15
   programming software, 13, 33
   wood routers, 9, 19
collaboration, in makerspaces, 6, 9, 11, 22, 26, 28
creativity, 5–6, 11, 15, 24, 26, 42

D

dongle, Square, 23
Dougherty, Dale, 4–5, 24
drills, 6
   drill press, 9, 15

E

Educate to Innovate, 5–6
efficiency, 27, 28, 37, 38, 43
engineering, 5–6, 24, 42, 55–56
   advanced degree in, 42
   associate's degree in, 42, 44
   classes in, 33
   design, 55–56
   industrial, 37, 46
   labs, 11
   logistics, 56

ABOUT THE AUTHOR

Jessica Shaw holds a BA in psychology from Texas State University. She has worked in human services and as a preschool teacher and currently enjoys writing nonfiction, fiction, and poetry for children and young adults.

PHOTO CREDITS

Cover (top), p. 1 Paul Taylor/The Image Bank/Getty Images; cover (bottom) gilaxia/E+/Getty Images; p. 5 gerasimov_foto_174/Shutterstock.com; pp. 8–9 Joerg Koch/Getty Images; p. 10 Sean Gallup/Getty Images; pp. 12, 20–21, 32–33, 40–41 Monkey Business Images/Shutterstock.com; p. 16 il21/Shutterstock.com; p. 18 sanjeri/E+/Getty Images; p. 25 David Gilder/Shutterstock.com; p. 27 Belish/Shutterstock.com; pp. 30–31 Hisayoshi Osawa/DigitalVision/Getty Images; p. 36 Everett Collection/Shutterstock.com; p. 45 Tzido Sun/Shutterstock.com; pp. 48–49 Jenson/Shutterstock.com; p. 50 © AP Images; p. 54 Tony Bock/Toronto Star/Getty Images; pp. 58–59 Wayhome Studio/Shutterstock.com; p. 62 fizkes/Shutterstock.com; p. 65 GaudiLab/Shutterstock.com; interior pages background (car manufacturing plant) Monty Rakusen/Cultura/Getty Images; back cover graphic Pobytov/DigitalVision Vectors/Getty Images; p. 4 illustration Bloomicon/Shutterstock.com.

Design and Layout: Michael Moy; Editor: Bethany Bryan; Photo Researcher: Nicole Reinholdt